Engravings Torn
from Insomnia

Engravings Torn from Insomnia

Selected Poems by
Olga Orozco

*Translation and Introduction
by Mary Crow*

BOA Editions, Ltd.   Rochester, NY   2002

First Edition
02 03 04 05 7 6 5 4 3 2 1

Publications by BOA Editions, Ltd.—
a not-for-profit corporation under section 501 (c) (3)
of the United States Internal Revenue Code—
are made possible with the assistance of grants from
the Literature Program of the New York State Council on the Arts,
the Literature Program of the National Endowment for the Arts,
the Sonia Raiziss Giop Charitable Foundation,
the Lannan Foundation,
as well as from the Mary S. Mulligan Charitable Trust,
the County of Monroe, NY, Citibank,
and the CIRE Foundation.

See page 104 for special individual acknowledgments.

Cover Design: Jean Brunel
Cover Art: "M. in the Water" by Roberto Lebron, acrylic on paper,
courtesy of the artist
Interior Design and Composition: Richard Foerster

BOA Logo: Mirko

LIBRARY OF CONGRESS CATALOGING-IN-PUBLICATION DATA

Orozco, Olga.
    Engraving torn from insomnia : poems / by Olga Orozco ; translated with an
introduction by Mary Crow.
        p. cm. — (The Lannan translations selection series ; no. 2)
    ISBN 1–929918–31–3 (alk. paper) — ISBN 1-929918-30-5 (pbk. : alk. paper)
    1. Orozco, Olga—Translations into English I. Crow, Mary II. Title. III. Series.

PQ7797.O6715 A23 2002
861'.64—dc21

                                                                    2002027924

BOA Editions, Ltd.
Steven Huff, Publisher
H. Allen Spencer, Chair
A. Poulin, Jr., President & Founder (1976–1996)
260 East Avenue, Rochester, NY 14604
www.boaeditions.org

CONTENTS

୬ **Introduction**   7

୬ **Part I**

El sello personal   14
Personal Stamp   15

Lejos, desde mi colina   18
Far Away, from My Hill   19

Plumas para unas alas   22
Some Feathers for My Wings   23

Cantos a Berenice, II   26
Songs to Berenice, II   27

Continente vampiro   28
Vampire Continent   29

୬ **Part II**

El presagio   34
Omen   35

Para destruir a la enemiga   36
To Destroy the Enemy   37

Remo contra la noche   40
I Row Against the Night   41

Para hacer un talismán   46
To Make a Talisman   47

୬ **Part III**

Un rostro en el otoño   50
A Face in Autumn   51

Les Jeux Sont Faits   52
Les Jeux Sont Faits   53

Después de los días   56
After Days   57

El extranjero   60
The Stranger   61

Catecismo animal   62
Animal Catechism   63

La abuela   66
The Grandmother   67

Part IV

Llega en cada tormenta   70
It Comes in Every Storm   71

El otro lado   72
The Other Side   73

Variaciones sobre el tiempo   74
Variations on Time   75

Olga Orozco   80
Olga Orozco   81

Part V

Las muertes   84
The Deaths   85

Balada de los lugares olvidados   86
Ballad of Forgotten Places   87

Muro de los lamentos   90
Wailing Wall   91

En el final era el verbo   92
In the End Was the Word   93

Chronological Placement of Poems
     in Orozco's Work   95
Acknowledgments   99
About the Author   100
About the Translator   101
Colophon   104

INTRODUCTION

Olga Orozco's poetic voice is as recognizable and unique as a fingerprint. No other poet anywhere in the world has a voice which sounds like hers. In a language that is a torrent of words, passionate and yearning, stumbling and pleading, Orozco's poems pour out an image-laden vision. Her poems seem to be called forth by shaman powers, out of a magical realm where primitive ritual, fairy tale, chaos, and nightmare mingle. Elements of the modern world float with fragments of dreams and tags of childhood recollections, making readers feel both dizzy and at home. Hers is a search for meaning and identity. Written in free verse, Orozco's poetry, as Jill S. Kuhnheim has said in *Gender, Politics, and Poetry in Twentieth Century Argentina*, "maintains a quality of ceremonial orality, making it a kind of ritualization of speech." Kuhnheim focuses her study, which she calls a "rereading of Argentina's literary heritage," on Orozco, a central figure in contemporary Argentine poetry, who died August 15, 1999.

Born in 1920 in Toay, near Buenos Aires, Orozco began her career on the fringes of the avant-garde in Argentina. She has been associated with the Argentine Surrealists and her work makes use of Surrealist techniques as well as the vatic voice of primitive poetry. Orozco's poetry, often compared to the poetry of early Modernist Olivero Girondo and to the work of Argentine Surrealists Enrique Molina and Alejandra Pizarnik, moves beyond surrealism in its metaphysical searching. One of her most frequent themes is an attempt to find God, meaning and purpose, in a cruel universe that is more Abyss than Eden. But Orozco is related not only to Argentine poetry. Her affinities to Spain's late Nobel Prize winner, Vicente Aleixandre, and his generation can be seen in both her subject matter and style, while her visits to Brazil and Europe have provided her poetry with a wide range of allusion to religion and literature.

Orozco is the author of almost twenty books (some of which are selections from previous books) that span more than 50 years and include volumes published in Spain, Mexico, Uruguay, and Colombia. Her nine principal collections of poetry began with *Desde Lejos* (*From Far Away*), which appeared in 1946, and ended with *Con esta boca, en este mundo* (*With This Mouth, in This World*) in 1992.

In addition, Orozco published two collections of short stories: *La oscuridad es otro sol* (*Darkness Is Another Sun*, 1967) and *También la luz es un abismo* (*Light Also Is an Abyss*, 1993 and 1995, enlarged edition). Widely featured in Argentine literary magazines and newspaper supplements, Orozco's poems have also appeared in magazines and newspapers in Sweden, Switzerland, Spain, France, Bolivia, Brazil, Chile, Colombia, Peru, Venezuela, Uruguay, Mexico, and the United States. They have been translated into French, English, Italian, German, Rumanian, Hindi, Portuguese, and Japanese.

Orozco won more than a dozen national, regional, or municipal prizes for her poetry, including the Premio Nacional de Poesia, Primer Premio de Poesia Fundacion Fortabat, and Premio Meridiano de Plata (Best Book of the Year), for *En el revés del cielo*, Premio Gabriela Mistral of the O.E.A. She received a grant from the Fondo Nacional de las Artes to study the occult and sacred in modern literature; she was unanimously selected to represent Argentina as candidate for an award for Spanish speaking writers offered by UNESCO. She also won major international awards including the Guadalajara prize for Latin American poetry and an award from the Italian Government to study the diverse currents of contemporary Italian poetry in the principal literary centers of that country. The University of Turin awarded her its Laurea de Poesía.

However, in spite of inclusion of her work in anthologies in Spain, Latin America, and the U.S., and in spite of critical articles that discuss her work in the context of her country's poetry, she has not yet been accorded the high place she deserves. Recent publication of interviews with her and of translations of her poems in literary magazines and anthologies should help establish her reputation in the U.S. Anthologies that have presented Orozco's work to readers in the U.S. include my own *Woman Who Has Sprouted Wings: Poems by Contemporary Latin American Women Poets* (1984 and 1987, second edition), *Women Poets of the World* (1983), *Contemporary Women Authors of Latin America* (1983), *Open to the Sun: A Bilingual Anthology of Latin-American Women Poets* (1979), and *Twentieth Century Latin American Poetry* (1996). Unfortunately, none of these anthologies includes more than a few of her poems.

Olga Orozco was one of the most obsessive of contemporary poets, returning again and again to certain themes, images, and words, and mulling over the significance of her experience as if she were a kabbalist reading the book of life and giving us her interpretations. Embedded in these interpretations we discover many events from Orozco's life even though her poems appear focused on a cosmic rather than a human realm. Simply put, Orozco was a thoroughly human poet in her suffering and in her passionate complaints and celebrations. As Venezuelan poet Juan Liscano has noted, "She's standing at the limit where night and day are confused, when it's dawn or dusk that's growing blue, as if an apparition from the beyond were drawing near, or a character from close by were stealing away."

But where she is "standing" in her poems is less a physical place than an interior space with the abyss around it, a place that is only one of the reoccurring "realities" in Orozco's poems. Another reality is the speaker's alternation between self as subject and object, or the dual selves in the poems, often wrestling with each other as she speaks through the "I" of the poem and also to a "you" who is beside or inside the "I." At times this struggle is located in the body, which is presented in Orozco's poetry as fragmented, inadequate, and with a will of its own which the "I" has difficulty directing. At other times the struggle seems to move out into the invisible world.

Or, again, Orozco locates the struggle in language which slips and slides in its torrent of several levels of meaning; it is a language that is veiled, embodying secrets and labyrinths. Thus, the intelligence speaking in a poem is confronted by many kinds of difficulties as she addresses her own internal split, the unknowable nature of the world she occupies, her sense of the fragmentation of her body, and her struggle to create meaning with words that may be decorations or signals or signs. Nonetheless, the poems, embedded in a dense imagery based in the phenomena of the physical world but giving rise to the visionary, represent the courage of the speaker's ongoing struggle and her plunge into that abyss where the struggle takes place and where poems arise.

The selection of Orozco's poems are my favorites from her generous body of work. I have arranged them so that the reader can grasp her main themes and obsessions. I chose *not* to order the poems chronologically because I felt that, in a short book, a more effective presentation would be small groupings of poems related through theme or language or imagery. For those who would like to read the poems chronologically I have included a list at the end of this volume that indicates the order of the poems' appearance in Orozco's major books of poems.

My deep gratitude goes to Olga Orozco for her suggestions on the wording of certain phrases in my translations and for her help in interpreting certain passages of her poetry. Several times in the years before her death, we met in her Buenos Aires apartment and her comments were extremely useful in my final revisions. I would also like to thank Meg Remple and Rebecca Davidson for reading and commenting on some of the translations, Marion Freeman for reading the Spanish and critiquing some of the translations, and Carol Christ for her work commenting on difficult passages and her typing as I completed the final draft. Finally, I owe more than I can repay to my late colleague and friend, Patsy Boyer, for reading my translations as they were drafted and again as this book took shape; her contributions were invaluable.

—Mary Crow

Engravings Torn
from Insomnia

I

EL SELLO PERSONAL

Estos son mis dos pies, mi error de nacimiento,
mi condena visible a volver a caer una vez
más bajo las implacables ruedas del zodíaco,
si no logran volar.
No son bases del templo ni piedras del hogar.
Apenas si dos pies, anfibios, enigmáticos,
remotos como dos serafines mutilados por la desgarradura del camino.
Son mis pies para el paso,
paso a paso sobre todos los muertos,
remontando la muerte con punta y con talón,
cautivos en la jaula de esta noche que debo atravesar y corre junto a mí.
Pies sobre brasas, pies sobre cuchillos,
marcados por el hierro de los Diez Mandamientos:
dos mártires anónimos tenaces en partir,
dispuestos a golpear en las cerradas puertas del planeta
y a dejar su señal de polvo y obediencia como una huella más,
apenas descifrable entre los remolinos que barren el umbral.
Pies dueños de la tierra,
pies de horizonte que huye,
pulidos como joyas al aliento del sol y al roce del guijarro:
dos pródigos radiantes royendo mi porvenir en los huesos del presente,
dispersando al pasar los rastros de ese reino prometido
que cambia de lugar y se escurre debajo de la hierba a medida que avanzo.
¡Qué instrumentos inaptos para salir y para entrar!
Y ninguna evidencia, ningún sello de predestinación bajo mis pies,
después de tantos viajes a la misma frontera.
Nada más que este abismo entre los dos,
esta ausencia inminente que me arrebata siempre hacia adelante,
y este soplo de encuentro y desencuentro sobre cada pisada.
¡Condición prodigiosa y miserable!
He caído en la trampa de estos pies
como un rehén del cielo o del infierno que se interroga en vano
        por su especie,
que no entiende sus huesos ni su piel,
ni esta perseverancia de coleóptero solo,

PERSONAL STAMP

These are my two feet, my error at birth,
and, if they cannot fly, a visible sentence
 to plunge once again
under the zodiac's relentless wheels.
They aren't pediments for a temple or stones for a hearth.
Just two feet, amphibian, enigmatic,
remote as two angels crippled by the road's crumbling.
They're two feet for the passage,
step by step over all the dead,
climbing toe and heel over death,
prisoners in this night's jail that runs beside me yet I must pass through.
My feet on burning coals, on knives,
branded by the iron of the Ten Commandments:
two anonymous martyrs stubbornly starting off,
prepared to bang on the planet's closed doors and leave
their mark of dust and obedience like one more trace
barely legible among the whirlwinds sweeping the threshold.
My feet, earth's masters,
feet of a fleeing horizon,
polished as jewels by the sun's breath and the cobblestones' touch:
two radiant prodigals gnawing my future in the present's bones,
scattering as they pass the signs of the promised land
that changes place, slipping beneath the grass, as I advance.
What useless instruments for exits and entrances!
And no evidence after so many journeys to the same frontier,
no stamp of predestination beneath my feet.
There's only this abyss between the two,
this imminent absence that drags me always onward
and this whisper of meeting and parting in every step.
Wonderful and miserable state!
I've fallen into the trap of these two feet
like a hostage of heaven or hell who asks in vain
        about her kind,
who can't understand her bones or her skin,
or even this perseverance like a solitary beetle's,

ni este tam-tam con que se le convoca a un eterno retorno.
¿Y adónde va este ser inmenso, legendario, increíble,
que despliega su vivo laberinto como una pesadilla,
aquí, todavía de pie,
sobre dos fugitivos delirios de la espuma, debajo del diluvio?

this drumming which summons her to an eternal return.
And where does this immense being go—legendary, incredible—
who unfolds her living labyrinth like a nightmare,
here, still standing,
on two delirious fugitives of foam, beneath the flood?

LEJOS, DESDE MI COLINA

A veces sólo era un llamado de arena en las ventanas,
una hierba que de pronto temblaba en la pradera quieta,
un cuerpo transparente que cruzaba los muros con blandura
dejándome en los ojos un resplandor helado,
o el ruido de una piedra recorriendo la indecible tiniebla
    de la medianoche;
a veces, sólo el viento.

Reconocía en ellos distantes mensajeros
de un país abismado con el mundo bajo las altas sombras
    de mi frente.
Yo los había amado, quizás, bajo otro cielo,
pero la soledad, las ruinas y el silencio eran siempre los mismos.
Más tarde, en la creciente noche,
miraba desde arriba la cabeza inclinada de una mujer vestida de congoja
que marchaba a través de todas sus edades como por un jardín
antiguamente amado.

Al final de sendero, antes de comenzar la durmiente planicie,
un brillo memorable, apenas un color pálido y cruel, la despedía;
y más allá no conocía nada.

¿Quién eras tú, perdida entre el follaje como las anteriores primaveras,
como alguien que retorna desde el tiempo a repetir los llantos,
los deseos, los ademanes lentos con que antaño entreabría sus días?

Sólo tú, alma mía.

Asomada a mi vida lo mismo que a una música remota,
para siempre envolvente,
escuchabas, suspendida quién sabe de qué muro de tierno desamparo,
el rumor apagado de las hojas sobre la juventud adormecida,
y elegías lo triste, lo callado, lo que nace debajo del olvido.

FAR AWAY, FROM MY HILL

Sometimes it was only a call of sand on the windows,
grass in the still meadow suddenly trembling,
a transparent body that softly passed through the walls
leaving an icy glow in my eyes,
or sometimes only the sound of a stone rolling
     over midnight's unspeakable darkness;
sometimes, only the wind.

I recognized in these things distant messengers
from a land submerged with the world
     under my forehead's high shadows.
Perhaps I had loved them under another sky,
but solitude, ruins, and silence remained always the same.
Later, in the growing night,
I looked from above at the bent head of a woman dressed in sorrow
who walked through all her ages as if through a garden
formerly loved.

At path's end, before the sleeping plains began,
a memorable shimmer, barely a pale and cruel color, bid her goodbye;
and, beyond, she recognized nothing.

Who were you, woman lost among foliage like earlier springtimes,
like someone who returns from time to repeat her cries,
desires, slow gestures with which yesterday she half-opened her days?

My soul, only you.

You appeared in my life as if in a distant music,
forever enveloping,
suspended from who knows what wall of tender homelessness,
listening to the leaves' stifled murmur over my sleepy youth,
and you chose the sad, the hushed, all that is born beneath oblivion.

¿En qué rincón de ti,
en qué desierto corredor resuenan los pasos clamorosos
    de una alegre estación,
el murmullo del agua sobre alguna pradera que prolangaba el cielo,
el canto esperanzado con que el amanecer corría a nuestro encuentro,
y también las palabras, sin duda tan ajenas al sitio señalado,
en las que agonizaba lo imposible?

Tú no respondes nada, porque toda respuesta de ti
    ha sido dada.

Acaso hayas vivido solamente
aquello que al arder no deja más que polvo de tristeza inmortal,
lo que saluda en ti, a través del recuerdo,
una eterna morada que al recibirnos se despide.

Tú no preguntas nada, nunca, porque no hay nadie ya que te responda.

Pero allá, sobre las colinas,
tu hermana, la memoria, con una rama joven aún entre las manos,
relata una vez más la leyenda inconclusa de un brumoso país.

In what corner of yourself,
in what deserted corridor do the clamorous steps of a happy season
        resound,
murmur of water in some meadow prolonging the sky,
hopeful song with which dawn ran to meet us,
and also words, no doubt as distant from the special place,
and in which the impossible was dying?

You don't respond at all, because any answer from you
        has already been given.

Perhaps you've lived everything, that burned,
leaves only dust of undying sadness,
or greets in you, through memory,
an eternal home simultaneously welcoming and abandoning us.

You don't ask anything, ever, because there's no one to answer you now.

But, over the hills,
your sister, memory, a young branch still in her hands,
tells once more the unfinished story of a misty country.

PLUMAS PARA UNAS ALAS

Un metro sesenta y cuatro de estatura sumergido en la piel
lo mismo que en un saco de obediencia y pavor.
Cautiva en esta piel,
cosida por un hilo sin nudo a esta ignorancia,
aferrada centímetro a centímetro a esta lisa envoltura que me protege
    a medias y por entero me delata,
siento la desnudez del animal,
el desabrido asombro del santo en el martirio,
la inexpresiva provocación al filo del cuchillo y al látigo del fuego.
No me sirve esta piel que apenas me contiene,
esta cáscara errante que me controla y me recuenta,
esta túnica avara cortada en lo invisible a la medida
    de mi muerte visible.
Apenas una pálida estría en la muralla:
la tensa cicatriz sobre la dentellada de la separación.
No puedo tocar fondo.
No consigo hacer pie dentro de esta membrana que me aparta de mí.
que me divide en dos y me vuelca al revés bajo las ruedas de los carros
    en llamas,
bajo espumas y labios y combates,
siempre a orillas del mundo, siempre a orillas del vértigo del alma.
No alcanza para lobo
y le falta también para cordero.
Y no obstante me escurro entre los dos bajo esta investidura
    del abismo,
invulnerable al golpe de mi sangre y a mi pira de huesos.
¿Quién apuesta su piel por esta piel ilesa e inconstante?
Nada para ganar.
Todo para perder en esta superficie donde solo se inscriben los errores
    sobre la borra de los años.
Y esa color de enigma que termina en pregunta,
ese urdimbre cerrada donde cruzan sus hilos la permanencia y la mudanza,
esa simulación de mansedumbre alrededor de un cuerpo irremediable,
ese aspecto de falso testimonio con que encubre, bajo la misma lona,
    el fantasma de ayer y el de mañana,

SOME FEATHERS FOR MY WINGS

Five-feet-four submerged in skin
as if in a sack of obedience and terror.
Captive in this skin
sewn by a knotless thread to ignorance,
bound inch by inch to this smooth wrapping that halfway protects me
    and wholly betrays me,
I feel the animal's nakedness,
the saint's unhappy surprise in his martyrdom,
inexpressible provocation at knife's edge and fire's whip.
It's worthless to me, this skin that barely contains me—
this wandering shell that controls and counts me again,
miserly tunic cut in the invisible to the measure
    of my visible death.
Hardly a pale groove on the wall:
tight scar over separation's bite.
I can't touch bottom.
I can't stand up inside this membrane that parts me from myself,
divides me in two and turns me inside out under the wheels
    of flaming chariots,
beneath foam and lips and battle,
always at world's edge, always at the edge of the soul's vertigo.
It fails short of wolf
but also fails as lamb.
Nevertheless I'm squeezed between the two in this ratifying
    of the abyss,
invulnerable to my blood's pounding and my bones' pyre.
Who risks his skin for this skin, untouched and inconstant?
Nothing to gain.
Everything to lose on this surface where only errors are inscribed
    on the lees of the years.
And that color of enigma which ends in a question,
that closed warp where permanence and change cross threads,
that pretense of meekness around an incurable body,
that aspect of false testimony which covers the ghosts of yesterday
    and tomorrow with the same sackcloth,

ese tacto como una chispa al sol, o un puñado de vidrios, o un huracán
    de mariposas,
¿a imagen de quién son?
¿A semejanza de qué dios migratorio fui arracada y envuelta
    en esta piel que exhala nostalgia?
Una mutilación de nubes y de plumas hacia la piel del cielo.

that touch like a spark in the sun, or a handful of glass, or a hurricane of
    butterflies—
whose images are they?
Like what migratory god was I uprooted and wrapped in this skin
    nostalgia exhales?
A mutilation of clouds and feathers toward the skin of heaven.

CANTOS A BERENICE, II

No estabas en mi umbral
ni yo salí a buscarte para colmar los huecos que fragua la nostalgia
y que presagian niños o animales hechos con la sustancia
      de la frustración.
Viniste paso a paso por los aires,
pequeña equilibrista en el tablón flotante sobre un foso de lobos
enmascarado por los andrajos radiante de febrero.
Venías condensándote desde la encandilada transparencia,
probándote otros cuerpos como fantasmas al revés,
como anticipaciones de tu eléctrica envoltura—
el erizo de niebla,
el globo de lustrosos vilanos encendidos,
la piedra imán que absorbe su fatal alimento,
la ráfaga emplumada que gira y se detiene alrededor de un ascua,
en torno de un temblor—.
Y ya habías aparecido en este mundo,
intacta en tu negrura inmaculada desde la cara hasta la cola,
más prodigiosa aún que el gato de Cheshire,
con tu porción de vida como una perla roja brillando entre los dientes.

SONGS TO BERENICE, II

You weren't there on my threshold,
nor did I go out looking for you to fill the hollows nostalgia forged,
hollows that foretell children or animals created
      out of frustration's substance.
Step by step you arrived through the air;
little tightrope walker on a plank floating above a pit of wolves,
masked in February's radiant tatters.
Condensing yourself out of dazzling transparency, you came
trying on other bodies as if they were ghosts inside out,
like anticipations of your electric wrapping—
sea urchin of mist,
globe of inflamed thistledown,
magnet absorbing its fatal food,
feathery gust that spins and stops circling an ember,
near a tremor—.
And already you had appeared in this world,
intact in your immaculate blackness from head to tail,
more marvelous even than the Cheshire cat,
with your portion of life like a red pearl shining between your teeth.

CONTINENTE VAMPIRO

No acerté con los pies sobre las huellas de mi ángel guardián.
Yo, que tenía tan bellos ojos en mi estación temprana,
no he sabido esquivar este despeñadero del destino que camina
     conmigo,
que se viste de luz a costa de mi desnudez y de mis duelos.
y que extiende su reino a fuerza de usurpaciones y rapiñas.

Es como un foso en marcha
al acecho de un paso en el vacío,
unas fauces que absorben esas escasas gotas de licor que dispensan
     los dioses,
un maldito anfiteatro en el que el viento aspira el porvenir de la heroína
y lo arroja a los leones
—su oro resonando al caer, grada tras grada, con sonido de muerte,
como suena el recuento al revés de todo gracia—.

Pegado a mis talones,
adherido a mis días como un cáncer a la urdimbre del tiempo,
tan fiel como el país natal o el sedimento ciego de mi herencia,
no solo se apodera de mis más denodadas, inseparables posesiones,
sino que se adelanta con su sombra veloz al vuelo de mi mano
y hasta se precipita contra el cristal azul que refleja el comienzo
     de un deseo.

A veces, muchas veces,
me acorrala contra el fondo de la noche cerrada, inapelable,
y despliega su cola, su abanico fastuoso como el rayo de un faro,
y exhibe uno por uno sus tesoros
—pedrerías hirientes a la luz de mis lágrimas:
la casa dibujada con una tiza blanca en todos los paraísos prometidos;
los duendes con sombreros de paja disipando la niebla en el jardín;
pedazos de inocencia para armar algún día su radiante cadáver;
mi abuela y Berenice en los altos desvanes de las aventuras infantiles;
mis padres, mis amigos, mis hermanos, brillando como lámparas
     en el túnel de las alamedas;

VAMPIRE CONTINENT

My feet couldn't catch up with my guardian angel's tracks,
and I, who had such beautiful eyes in my early season,
still haven't learned how to avoid destiny's precipice that travels
     with me,
dresses in light at the price of my nakedness and pain,
and expands its realm through seizure and pillage.

It's like a grave marching
to ambush my passage into emptiness,
like a maw that drinks in the few drops of liquor the gods
     offer,
like a cursed amphitheater where the wind sucks in the heroine's future
and throws it to the lions—
her gold echoing as it falls, bit by bit, the sound of death
as a final reckoning peals as if it were all kindness inside out—.

It sticks to my heels,
clings to my days as a cancer clings to time's warp,
faithful as my birthplace or the blind sediment of my heritage—
not only seizing my most insistent, inseparable belongings,
but also advancing with its swift shadow to the flight of my hand
and even hurling itself against the blue glass reflecting
     a desire's beginning.

Sometimes, often,
it corners me at the back of deepest night, and, allowing no appeal,
uncoils its tail, fan splendid as a lighthouse beam,
and, one by one, exhibits its treasures—
jewels wounded by my tears' light:
a house sketched with white chalk in all the promised paradises;
ghosts in straw hats dissipating the mist in the garden;
bits of innocence for building a radiant corpse some day;
my grandmother and Berenice in the high attics of childhood adventures;
my parents, friends, brothers and sisters, shining like lamps
     in the tunnel of elm groves;

vitrales de los grandes amores arrancados a la catedral de la esperanza;
ropajes de la dicha doblados para otra vez en el arcón sin fondo;
las barajas del triunfo entresacadas de unos naipes marcados;
y piedras prodigiosas, estampas iluminadas, y ciudades como luciérnagas
      del bosque,
todo, todo, sobre una red de telarañas rojas
que son en realidad caminos que se cruzan con las venas cortadas.

No hablo aquí de ganancias y de pérdidas,
de victorias fortuitas y derrotas.
No he venido a llorar con agónicos llantos mi desdicha,
mi balance de polvo,
sino a afirmar la sede de la negación:
esta vieja cantera de codicias,
este inmenso ventisquero vampiro que se viste de luces
      con mi duelo.

Y yo como una proa de navío pirata,
península raída llevando un continente de saqueos.

showcases of great loves snatched from the cathedral of hope;
trappings of joy folded to go back into the bottomless chest;
decks of triumph selected from a few marked cards;
and prodigious stones, colored pictures, cities like fireflies
     in the forest—
all, all, above a net of red spiderwebs
that are, in reality, intersecting roads with their veins cut.

I'm not speaking here of profit and losses,
of fortuitous victories and defeats.
I haven't come to cry over my misfortune with anguished weeping,
or over my balance of dust,
but to affirm the seat of denial:
this ancient quarry of greed,
this glacier, immense and vampire, that dons a suit of lights made
     of my pain.

And me like the prow of a pirate ship,
worn-out peninsula bearing a plundered continent.

II

EL PRESAGIO

Estaba escrito en sombras.
Fue trazado con humo en medio de dos alas de colores,
casi una incrustación de riguroso luto cortando en dos el brillo
        de la fiesta.
Lo anunció muchas veces el quejido escarchado del cristal debajo
        de tus pies.
Lo dijeron oscuros personajes girando siempre a tientas,
porque nunca hay salido para nadie en los vertiginosos albergues
        de los sueños.
Lo propagó la hierba que fue un áspero, tenebroso plumaje una mañana.
Lo confirmaron día tras día las fisuras súbitas en los muros,
los trazos de carbón sobre la piedra, las arañas traslúcidas, los vientos.
Y de repente se desbordó la noche,
rebasó en la medida del peligro las vitrinas cerradas, los lazos ajustados,
las manos que a duras penas contenían la presión tormentosa.
Un gran pájaro negro cayó sobre tu plato.
Es como la envoltura de algún fuego sombrío, taciturno, sofocado,
que vino desde lejos horadando al pasar la intacta protección de cada día.
Ahora observas humear esa cosecha escalofriante.
Llega desde las más remotas plantaciones de tu presentimiento
        y de tu miedo,
llega incesantemente exhalando el misterio.
Está sobre tu plato y no hay distancia alguna que te aparte,
ni escondite posible.

OMEN

It was written in shadows.
It was outlined with smoke between two colored wings,
almost an incrustation of strict mourning cutting the celebration's glow
    in two.
The frosty complaint of glass beneath your feet announced it
    often.
Dark characters whirling blindly forever said it
because there is no exit ever for anyone in the dizzying den
    of dreams.
Harsh shadowy plumage, the grass spread it one morning.
Sudden splits in the walls confirmed it day after day,
charcoal traces on stone, transparent spiders, winds.
And suddenly when night spilled over,
it dangerously overflowed the closed showcases, tight knots,
hands that could hardly hold the stormy pressure.
A great black bird fell onto your plate.
Like wrapping around some fire—dark, taciturn, breathless—
it came from far away, piercing as it passed the pure skin of every day.
Now you notice how this chilling harvest smokes.
How it comes from the most remote plantations of your foreboding
    and fear,
arrives endlessly exhaling mystery.
It's on your plate and there's no distance between you,
no hiding-place possible.

PARA DESTRUIR LA ENEMIGA

Mira a la que avanza desde el fondo del agua borrando el día
    con sus manos,
vaciando en piedra gris lo que tú destinabas a memoria de fuego,
cubriendo de cenizas las más bellas estampas prometidas
    por las dos caras de los sueños.
Lleva sobre su rostro la señal:
ese color de invierno deslumbrante que nace donde mueres,
esas sombras como de grandes alas que barren desde siempre
    todos los juramentos del amor.

Cada noche, a lo lejos, en esa lejanía donde el amante duerme
    con los ojos abiertos a otro mundo adonde nunca llegas,
ella cambia tu nombre por el ruido más triste de la arena;
tu voz, por un sollozo sepultado en el fondo de la canción que nadie
    ya recuerda;
tu amor, por una estéril ceremonia donde se inmola el crimen
    y el perdón.
Cada noche, en el deshabitado lugar adonde vueles,
ella pone a secar la cifra de tu edad al bajar la marea,
o cose con el hilo de tus días la noche del adiós,
o prepara con el sabor del tiempo más hermoso ese turbio brebaje
    que paladeas en la soledad,
ese ardiente veneno que otros llaman nostalgia
y que tan lentamente transforma el corazón en un puñado
    de semillas amargas.

No la dejes pasar.
Apaga su camino con la hoguera del árbol partido por el rayo.
Arroja su reflejo donde corran las aguas para que nunca vuelva.
Sepulta la medida de su sombra debajo de tu casa para que por su boca
    la tierra la reclame.
Nómbrala con el nombre de lo deshabitado.
Nómbrala.
Nómbrala con el frío y el ardor,
con la cera fundida como una nieve sucia donde cae la forma de su vida,

TO DESTROY THE ENEMY

Look at the woman who approaches from the water's depth
    erasing the day with her hands,
emptying what you'd destined for fire's memory into gray stone,
covering with ash the most beautiful pictures promised
    by the two faces of dream.
She bears the sign on her face:
that color of dazzling winter born where you die,
those shadows as if of great wings that sweep away forever every vow
    of love.

Each night, in the distance, that distance where the lover sleeps
    with eyes open to another world where you never arrive,
she exchanges your name for sand's saddest sound;
your voice, for a sob buried in the depth of a song no one remembers
    any longer;
your love, for a barren ceremony in which crime and pardon
    are burned.
Each night, in the deserted place you return to,
when the tide ebbs she puts the cipher of your age out to dry,
or sews gooodbye's night with the thread of your days,
or prepares that turbid drink you savor in solitude with the flavor
    of the most beautiful time,
that burning poison others call nostalgia
and which is so slowly transforming your heart into a fistful
    of bitter seeds.

Don't let her pass.
Cut off her path with a wildfire from the tree split by lightning.
Cast her reflection where the waters run so she can never return.
Bury her shadow's length under your house so earth can reclaim her
    through its mouth.
Name her with the name of the deserted.
Name her.
Name her with cold and burning,
with wax melted like dirty snow where her life's form falls,

con las tijeras y el puñal,
con el rastro de la alimaña herida sobre la piedra negra,
con el humo del ascua,
con la fosa del imposible amor abierta al rojo vivo en su costado,
con la palabra de poder
nómbrala y mátala.

Y no olvides sepultar la moneda.
Hacia arriba la noche bajo el pasado párpado del invierno más largo.
Hacia abajo la efigie y la inscripción:
"Reina de las espadas,
Dama de las desdichas,
Señora de las lágrimas:
en el sitio en que estés con dos ojos te miro,
con tres nudos te ato,
la sangre te bebo
y el corazón te parto."

Si miras otra vez en el fondo del vaso,
sólo verás ahora una descolorida cicatriz cuyos bordes se cierran donde
   se unen las aguas,
pero pueden abrirse en otra herida, adonde nadie sabe.

Porque ella te fue anunciada en el séptimo día
—en el día primero de tu culpa—,
y asumiste su nombre con el tuyo,
con los nombres vacíos, con el amor y con el número,
con el mismo collar de sal amarga que anuda la condena a tu garganta.

with scissors and dagger,
the wounded animal's track across black rock,
ember's smoke,
with the grave of impossible love open to the red fire in her side,
with the word of power,
name her and kill her.

And don't forget to bury the coin.
Face up, the night under the heavy eyelid of the longest winter.
Face down, the effigy and the inscription:
"Queen of swords,
Mistress of grief,
Lady of tears:
Wherever you are, I look at you with both eyes,
I tie you with three knots,
I drink your blood
and I split your heart."

If you look again into the bottom of the glass,
you will see only a discolored scar whose edges close where the waters
      join,
yet open into another wound, in a place nobody knows.

Because she was announced to you on the seventh day—
the first day of your guilt—
and you took her name with yours,
with the empty names, with love and with number,
with the very chain of bitter salt that fastens the death sentence around
      your throat.

REMO CONTRA LA NOCHE

Apaga ya la luz de ese cuchillo, madrastra de las sombras.
No necesito luces para mirar en el abismo de mi sangre,
en el naufragio de mi raza.
Apágala, te digo;
apágala contra tu propia cara con este soplo frío con que vuela
　　mi madre.
Y tú, criatura ciega, no dejes escapar la soga que nos lleva.

Yo remonto la noche junto a ti.
Voy remando contigo desde tu nacimiento
con un fardo de espinas y esta campana inútil en las manos.

Están sordos allá.
Ninguna pluma de ángel,
ningún fulgor del cielo hemos logrado con tantas migraciones
　　arrancadas al alma.

Nada más que este viaje en la tormenta
a favor de unas horas inmóviles en ti, usurera del alba;
nada más que este insomnio en la corriente,
por un puñado de ascuas,
por un par de arrasados corazones,
por un jirón de piel entre tus dientes fríos.

Pequeño, tú vuelves a nacer.
Debes seguir creciendo mientras corre hacia atrás la borra de estos años,
y yo escarbo la lumbre en el tapiz
donde algún paso tuyo fue marcado por un carbón aciago,
y arranco las raíces que te cubren los pies.

Hay tanta sombra aquí por tan escasos días,
tantas caras borradas por los harapos de la dicha
para verte mejor,
tantos trotes de lluvias y alimañas en la rampa del sueño
para oírte mejor,

I ROW AGAINST THE NIGHT

Put out the light of that knife now, stepmother of darkness.
I don't need light to see into my blood's abyss,
into the shipwreck of my kind.
Put it out, I tell you,
put it out against your own face with this cold breath with which my
        mother flies.
And you, blind child, don't let go of the rope that carries us on.

I climb the night beside you.
I've been paddling with you ever since your birth,
a bundle of thorns in my hands and this useless bell.

They're all deaf there.
We haven't managed to get a single angel feather,
a single sky shine with so many migrations torn
        from our souls.

Only this trip in the storm
for a few hours motionless in you, usuress of dawn;
only this insomnia in the current,
for a fistful of embers,
for a couple of ravaged hearts,
for a strip of skin between your cold teeth.

Little one, you're born again.
You ought to go on growing while the waste of these years runs backward
and I rake the fire in the tapestry
where some step of yours was marked by a fateful hot coal,
and I tear out the roots that cover your feet.

There's so much darkness here for your short lifetime,
so many faces erased by the shreds of happiness,
the better to see you,
so much rushing of rain and vermin on the ramp of sleep,
the better to hear you,

tantos carros de ruinas que ruedan con el trueno
para moler mejor tus huesos y los míos,
para precipitar la bolsa de guijarros en el despeñadero de la bruma
y ponernos a hervir,
lo mismo que en los cuentos de la vieja hechicera.

Pequeño, no mires hacia atrás: son fantasmas del cielo.
No cortes esa flor: es el rescoldo vivo del infierno.
No toques esas aguas: son tan sólo la sed que se condensa en lágrimas
     y en duelo.
No pises esa piedra que te hiere con la menuda sal
      de todos estos años.
No pruebes ese pan porque tiene el sabor de la memoria y es áspero
     y amargo.
No gires con la ronda en el portal de las apariciones,
no huyas con la luz, no digas que no estás.

Ella trae una aguja y un puñal,
tejedora de escarchas.
Te anuda para bordar la duración o te arrebata al filo
      de un relámpago.
Se esconde en una nuez,
se disfraza de lámpara que cae en el desván o de puerta que se abre
      en el estanque.
Corroe cada edad,
convierte los espejos en un nido de agujeros,
con los dientes veloces para la mordedura como un escalofrío,
como el anuncio de tu porvenir en este día que detiene el pasado.

Señora, el que buscas no está.
Salió hace mucho tiempo de cara a la avaricia de la luz,
y esa espalda obstinada de pródigo sin padres para el regreso
     y el perdón,
y esos pies indefensos con que echaba a rodar las últimas monedas.
¿A quién llamas, ladrona de miserias?
El ronquido que escuchas es tan sólo el del trueno perdido en el jardín
y esa respiración es el jadeo de algún pobre animal que escarba
     la salida.
No hay ninguna migaja para ti, roedora de arenas.

so many chariots of ruins rolling with thunder,
the better to grind your bones and mine,
to drop the bag of stones into the misty abyss
and set us boiling,
just as in the stories of the old witch.

Little one, don't look back: they're ghosts from heaven.
Don't cut that flower: it's hell's living ember.
Don't touch those waters: only thirst condensed into tears
        and pain.
Don't step on that stone which wounds you with the fine salt
        of all those years.
Don't sample that bread because it tastes of memory, sharp
        and bitter.
Don't spin around in the portal of apparitions,
don't flee with the light, don't say you aren't here.

A weaver of frost,
she bears both needle and dagger.
She knots you in order to embroider time or snatches you
        from lightning's edge.
She's hidden in a nut,
disguised as a lamp that falls in the attic or as a doorway that opens
        in the pool.
She chews every age,
turns mirrors into a nest of holes,
with her teeth as quick to bite as a chill,
like the sign of your future on this day that halts your past.

Lady, the one you look for isn't here.
He left long ago facing light's avarice
with that stubborn shoulder of a prodigal son who has no parents
        for his return and pardon,
and with those defenseless feet that set his last coins rolling.
Thief of miseries, who are you calling?
The snore you hear is only thunder lost in the garden,
and that breath only the panting of some poor animal scratching
        at the exit.
Sand's rat, there's no crumb for you.

Este frío no es tuyo.
Es un frío sin nadie que se dejó olvidado no sé quién.

Criatura, esta es sólo una historia de brujas y de lobos,
estampas arrancadas al insomnio de remotas abuelas.
Y ahora, ¿adónde vas con esta soga inmóvil que nos lleva?
¿Adónde voy en esta barca sola contra el revés del cielo?
¿Quién me arroja desde mi corazón como una piedra ciega
        contra oleajes de piedra
y abre unas roncas alas que restallan igual que una bandera?

Silencio. Está pasando la nieve de otro cuento entre tus dedos.

This cold isn't yours.
It's an empty cold forgotten by no one knows who.

Child, this is only a story of witches and wolves,
engravings torn from the insomnia of distant grandmothers.
And now, where are you going with this still rope that carries us on?
Where am I going in this boat, alone against heaven's other side?
Who throws me out of my own heart like a blind stone
      against stone waves
and unfolds roaring wings that beat like a flag?

Silence. The snow of another story is slipping through your fingers.

PARA HACER UN TALISMÁN

Se necesita sólo tu corazón
hecho a la viva imagen de tu demonio o de tu dios.
Un corazón apenas, como un crisol de brasas para la idolatría.
Nada más que un indefenso corazón enamorado.
Déjalo a la intemperie,
donde la hierba aúlle sus endechas de nodriza loca
y no pueda dormir,
donde el viento y la lluvia dejen caer su látigo en un golpe de azul escalofrío
sin convertirlo en mármol y sin partirlo en dos,
donde la oscuridad abra sus madrigueras a todas las jaurías
y no logre olvidar.
Arrójalo después desde lo alto de su amor al hervidero de la bruma.
Ponlo luego a secar en el sordo regazo de la piedra,
y escarba, escarba en él con una aguja fría hasta arrancar el último grano
      de esperanza.
Deja que lo sofoquen las fiebres y la ortiga,
que lo sacuda el trote ritual de la alimaña,
que lo envuelva la injuria hecha con los jirones de sus antiguas glorias.
Y cuando un día un año lo aprisione con la garra de un siglo,
antes que sea tarde,
antes que se convierta en momia deslumbrante,
abre de par en par y una por una todas sus heridas:
que las exhiba al sol de la piedad, lo mismo que el mendigo,
que plaña su delirio en el desierto,
hasta que sólo el eco de un nombre crezca en él con la furia
      del hambre:
un incesante golpe de cuchara contra el plato vacío.
Si sobrevive aún,
si ha llegado hasta aquí hecho a la viva imagen de tu demonio o de tu dios;
he ahí un talismán más inflexible que la ley,
más fuerte que las armas y el mal del enemigo.
Guárdalo en la vigilia de tu pecho igual que a un centinela.
Pero vela con él.
Puede crecer en ti como la mordedura de la lepra;
puede ser tu verdugo.
¡El inocente monstruo, el insaciable comensal de tu muerte!

TO MAKE A TALISMAN

All you need is your heart
made in the living image of your demon or your god.
Only it, like a crucible of red-hot coals for idolatry.
Nothing more than a helpless and lovesick heart.
Leave it out in the elements,
where the grass howls dirges like a crazy nurse
and it can't sleep,
where the whip of wind and rain falls on it in blows of blue chill
without turning it into marble or breaking it in two,
where darkness opens dens to every pack of beasts
and it cannot forget.
Afterwards hurl your heart from the summit of its love into the roiling fog.
Then spread it out to dry on the deaf lap of stone,
and scratch, scratch it with a cold needle till you rip out the last grain
        of hope.
Let fevers and nettles suffocate it,
let the beast's ritual rush jolt it,
let insult made with the tatters of its former glories wrap it round.
And when, some day, some year your heart is captured by the century's claws,
before it turns into a shocking mummy,
before it's too late:
let it open wide its wounds one by one,
let it display them as a beggar would to the sun of mercy;
let it moan its delirium in the desert,
until only the echo of a name grows within it summoning the fury
        of hunger:
an endless tapping of a spoon against an empty plate.
If your heart still survives,
if it has come this far as the living image of your demon or your god;
it will be a talisman more inflexible than the law,
stronger than weapons and the enemy's malice.
Guard it in your breast's vigil like a sentinel.
But keep watch with it.
It can grow in you like the bite of leprosy;
it can become your executioner.
Innocent monster, insatiable guest at your death!

III

UN ROSTRO EN EL OTOÑO

La mujer del otoño llegaba a mi ventana
sumergiendo su rostro entre las vides,
reclinando sus hombros, sus vegetales hombros, en las nieblas,
buscando inútilmente su pecho resignado a nacer y morir
      entre dos sueños.

Desde un lejano cielo la aguardaban las lluvias,
aquellas que golpeaban duramente su dulce piel labrada por el duelo
      de una vieja estación,
sus ojos que nacían desde el llanto
o su pálida boca perdida para siempre, como en una plegaria
      que inconmovibles dioses acallaran.

Luego estaban los vientos adormeciendo el mundo entre sus manos,
repitiendo en sus mustios cabellos enlazados
la inacabable endecha de las hojas que caen;
y allá, bajo las frías coronas del invierno,
el cálido refugio de la tierra para su soledad, semejante a un presagio,
retornada a su estela como un ala.

Oh, vosotros, los inclementes ángeles del tiempo,
los que habitáis aún la lejanía
—ese olvido demasiado rebelde—;
vosotros, que lleváis a la sombra,
a sus marchitos ídolos, eternos todavía,
mi corazón hostil, abandonado:
no me podréis quitar esta pequeña vida entre dos sueños,
este cuerpo de lianas y de hojas que cae blandamente,
que se muere hacia adentro, como mueren las herbas.

A FACE IN AUTUMN

The autumn woman came to my window
sinking her face into the grapevines,
hunching her shoulders, her vegetal shoulders, into the mists,
uselessly searching her heart resigned to being born and dying
    between two dreams.

Rains from a distant sky waited for her,
rains that cruelly struck her sweet skin engraved by an old season's
    mourning,
her eyes born from crying,
or her pale mouth forever lost as if in a prayer silenced
    by implacable gods.

Then came the wind lulling the world in her hands,
repeating the endless dirge of falling leaves
in her gloomy bound hair;
and beyond, beneath winter's cold funeral wreaths,
she returned to her wake like a wing,
warm earthy refuge for her solitude, an omen.

Oh, you, the inclement angels of time,
who still live in the distance—
that oblivion which is too rebellious—
you, who carry my abandoned and angry heart off to the darkness,
to its withered idols, still eternal:
you cannot take from me this little life between two dreams,
this body of vines and leaves that is falling tenderly,
dying inside, the way the grass dies.

LES JEUX SONT FAITS

¡Tanto esplendor en este día!
¡Tanto esplendor inútil, vacío, traicionado!
¿Y quién te dijo acaso que vendrían por ti días dorados
      en años venideros?
Días que dicen sí, como luces que zumban, como lluvias sagradas.
¿Acaso bajó el ángel a prometerte un venturoso exilio?
Tal vez hasta pensaste que las aguas lavaban los guijarros
para que murmuraran tu nombre por las playas,
que a tu paso florecerían porque sí las retamas
y las frases ardientes velarían insomnes en tu honor.
Nada me trae el día.
No hay nada que me aguarde más allá del final de la alameda.
El tiempo se hizo muro y no puedo volver.
Aunque ahora supiera dónde perdí las llaves y confundí
      las puertas
o si fue solamente que me distrajo el vuelo de algún pájaro,
por un instante, apenas, y tal vez ni siquiera,
no puedo reclamar entre los muertos.
Todo lo que recuerda mi boca fue borrado de la memoria de otra boca;
se alojó en nuestro abrazo la ceniza, se nos precipitó la lejanía,
y soy como la sobreviviente pompeyana
separada por los siglos del amante sepultado en la piedra.
Y de pronto este día que fulgura
como un negro telón partido por un tajo, desde ayer, desde nunca.
¡Tanto esplendor y tanto desamparo!
Sé que la luz delata los territorios de la sombra y vigila
      en suspenso,
y que oscuridad exalta el fuego y se arrodilla en los rincones.
Pero, ¿cuál de las dos labra el legítimo derecho de la trama?
Ah, no se trata de triunfo, de aceptación ni de sometimiento.
Yo me pregunto, entonces:
más tarde o más temprano, mirado desde arriba,
¿cuál es en el recuento final, el verdadero, intocable destino?
¿El que quise y no fue? ¿el que no quise y fue?

LES JEUX SONT FAITS*

So much splendor on this day!
So much useless splendor, empty and betrayed!
And who perhaps told you that golden days would arrive for you
    in coming years?
Days that say yes, like lights which buzz, like sacred rain.
Perhaps the angel came down to promise you a happy exile?
Perhaps you even thought that waters washed the stones
so they would speak your name on the beaches,
that at your step of course the broom would blossom
and burning sentences would stand guard insomniac in your honor.
The day brings me nothing.
There's nothing that waits for me beyond the end of the park.
Time turned into a wall and I cannot return.
Even though I knew already where I lost the keys and confused one
    door with another,
or even though I was distracted only by the flight of some bird,
for an instant, barely, and perhaps not even that,
I can't file a complaint among the dead.
All my mouth remembers was erased from the memory of another mouth;
ash lodged itself in our embrace, distance brought about our downfall,
and I'm like a survivor of Pompeii
separated by centuries from my lover buried in stone.
Then suddenly today flashes
like a black curtain split by a slash since yesterday, since forever.
So much splendor and so much abandonment!
I know that light betrays the territories of shadows and keeps watch
    in suspense,
and that darkness exalts the fire and falls on its knees in corners.
But which of the two traces the true course of the plot?
Ah, it's not about triumph, acceptance, or submission.
I ask myself, then:
later or earlier, seen from above,
which is in the final reckoning, the true, untouchable destiny?
The one I wanted who didn't exist? The one I didn't want who did?

*The game is up.

Madre, madre,
vuelve a erigir la casa y bordemos la historia.
Vuelve a contar mi vida.

Mother, mother,
come back to rebuild our house and let's embroider our story.
Return to tell my life once more.

DESPUÉS DE LOS DÍAS

Será cuando el misterio de la sombra,
piadosa madre de mi cuerpo, haya pasado;
cuando las angustiadas palomas, mis amigas, no repitan por mí
    su vuelo funerario;
cuando el último brillo de mi boca se apague duramente, sin orgullo;
mucho después del llanto de la muerte.

No acabarás entonces,
mitad de mi vida fatigada de cantar lo terrestre.
Nadie podrá mirarte con esa misma pena que se tiene al mirar
    un pálido arenal interminable,
porque tú volverás, ¡oh corazón amante del recuerdo!, a las tristes
    planicies.

Serás el mismo viento tormentoso de agosto,
huracanado y redentor como la plegaria de un tiempo arrepentido;
serás, cuando la noche, esa visión luciente que responde en la niebla
a una señal de oscuro desamparo;
tu voz tendrá un sonido humilde y temeroso
porque será el rumor doliente de los cercos que guardaron
    tu infancia,
al desmoronarse;
y tu color será el color del aire, dulcemente amarillo,
que las hojas de otoño desvanecen para sobrevivir.

Detrás de las paredes que limitan los sueños
estarían todavía los hombres
prisioneros de sus mismos semblantes,
aquéllos, los marchitos,
los que dicen adiós con su mirada única
a cada nuevo paso del sombrío cortejo de su sangre,
mientras van consumiendo su destino de arena porque su cielo cabe
    en una lágrima.

AFTER DAYS

It will happen when the shadow's mystery,
merciful mother of my body, has passed;
when my friends, the anguished doves, no longer repeat their funeral
    flight for me;
when my mouth's final shine is extinguished, harshly, without pride;
long after the weeping for death.

You—that half of my life weary of singing the earthly—
will not end then.
No one will be able to look at you with that same suffering we feel
    when looking at pale endless sands,
because you will return—oh, heart, lover of memory!—to the sad
    plains!

You'll be that very stormy wind of August,
hurricane and savior, like a prayer from a repentant time;
you'll exist when night does, that shining vision which answers in the mist
to a signal of dark helplessness;
your voice will have a humble and fearful sound
because it will be the aching rumor of the fences that sheltered
    your childhood
gradually crumbling away;
and your color will be the color of air, the sweet yellow
autumn leaves fade to in order to survive.

Behind the walls limiting dreams
there will still be men,
prisoners of their own faces,
the withered ones,
saying goodbye with a unique glance
at each new step of their blood's shadowy procession,
while they gradually wear away their destiny of sand because their sky
    fits into a single tear.

No te detengas, no, glorioso mediodía de mis huesos.
Ellos ven en el polvo un letárgico olvido tan largo como el mundo,
y tú sabes, cuerpo mío dichoso desde el tiempo,
que no en vano mecieron tu corazón las lentas primaveras,
que tu pecho está unido a ese incesante aliento que reconoce en él
    una guarida,
que será necesario morir para vivir el canto glorioso de la tierra.

Glorious noon of my bones, don't stop, no.
My bones see in the dust a lethargic forgetfulness as wide as the world,
and you know, my happy body beyond time,
that the slow springtimes didn't rock your heart in vain,
that your heart is joined to that incessant spirit which recognizes in it
    a lair,
for it will be necessary to die in order to live the earth's glorious song.

EL EXTRANJERO

El pasó entre vosotras,
gentes amables como el calor del fuego en la choza vecina.
Mas ¿qué fue vuestro acento sino un puñal mellado que vacila
    en la hondura del pecho?
Él os miró pasar,
días adormilados como bestias en sumisas praderas.
Mas ¿qué fue vuestra paz sino arenas ardiendo debajo de los párpados?
Lejos corría el viento que no deja salobres las mejillas.
Lejos hay un lugar para su sombra junto a la fresca sombra
    de los antepasados.
Lejos será el ausente menos ausente ahora.
¡Oh! Secad vuestras lágrimas
que nada son para la sed del extranjero.
Guardad vuestras plegarias:
él no pedía amor ni otro exilio en el cielo.
Y dejad que la tierra levante sus arrullos de injuriada madrastra:
"Yo guardo un corazón tan áspero y hostil como la hoja de la higuera".

THE STRANGER

He passed among you,
people kindly as the fire's warmth in a neighboring hut.
But what was your accent except a jagged dagger quivering
      in the depth of his breast?
He watched you pass,
days drowsy as beasts in humble pastures.
But what was your peace except sand burning under his eyelids?
Far away the wind blew leaving no cheeks salty.
Far away a place exists for his shade beside the fresh shades
      of his ancestors.
Far away he will be the absent one less absent now.
Oh, dry your tears
that do not quench the thirst of the stranger.
Keep your prayers:
he didn't ask for love or any other heavenly exile.
And let earth lift up its lullabies like an insulted stepmother:
"I bear a heart as harsh and angry as the leaf of the fig tree."

CATECISMO ANIMAL

Somos duros fragmentos arrancados del reverso del cielo,
trozos como cascotes insolubles
vueltos hacia este muro donde se inscribe el vuelo de la realidad,
la mordedura blanca del destierro hasta el escalofrío.
Suspendidos en medio del derrumbe por obra del error,
enfrentamos de pie las inclemencias, la miserable condición del rehén,
expuestos del costado que se desgasta al roce de la arena y al golpe del azar,
bajo el precario sol que quizás hoy se apague, que no salga
     mañana.
No tenemos ni marca de predestinación ni vestigios de las primaveras luces:
ni siquiera sabemos qué soplo nos expulsa y nos aspira.
Apenas si el sabor de la sed, si la manera de traspasar la niebla,
si esta vertiginosa sustancia en busca de salida,
hablan de alguna parte donde las mutiladas visiones se completan,
donde se cumple Dios.
Ah descubrir la imagen oculta e impensable del reflejo,
la palabra secreta, el bien perdido,
la otra mitad que siempre fue una nube inalcanzable desde la soledad
y es toda la belleza que nos ciñe en su trama y nos rehace,
una mirada eterna como un lago para sumergir el amor
     en su versión insomne,
en su asombro dorado.
Pero no hay quien divise el centelleo de una sola fisura para poder pasar.
Nunca con esta vida que no alcanza para ir y volver,
que reduce las horas y oscila contra el viento,
que se retrae y vibra como llama aterida cuando asoma la muerte.
Nunca con este cuerpo donde siempre tropieza el universo.
Él quedará incrustado en este muro.
Él será más opaco que un pedrusco roído por la lluvia hasta el juicio final.
¿Y servirá este cuerpo más allá para sobrevivir,
el inepto monarca, el destronado, el frágil desertor obligatorio,
rescatado otra vez desde su nadie, desde las entrañas de un escorial
     de brumas?

ANIMAL CATECHISM

We are hard fragments torn from heaven's other side,
chunks like insoluble rubble
turned toward this wall inscribed with reality's flight—
white bite of exile to the cold.
Suspended in the middle of the avalanche by mistake,
we face the storms standing, exposed, hostage's miserable state,
with our flank worn down by sand's friction and chance's blow,
beneath the precarious sun that may go out today, may not rise
    tomorrow.
We have neither predestination's mark nor the vestiges of first light;
we don't even know what gust expels us and inhales us.
We scarcely know if the taste of thirst, if a way of penetrating the fog,
if this dizzying substance in search of outlet,
speak of some place where mutilated visions are completed,
where God is fulfilled.
Ah to discover reflection's hidden and unthinkable image,
the secret word, the lost good,
the other half that always was a cloud unreachable from solitude
and is all the beauty that binds us in its plot and recreates us,
an eternal glance like a lake for submerging love
    in its insomniac version,
in its golden surprise.
But there's no one to see the glimmer of a single crack to slip through.
Never with this life that's not enough for going and returning,
that shrinks the hours and wavers against the wind,
takes refuge when death appears, flickering like a flame shivering with cold.
Never with this body where the universe always stumbles.
It will remain encrusted in this wall,
more opaque than a boulder gnawed by rain till the last judgment.
And will this body be of use for surviving in the beyond—
an inept and dethroned monarch, a fragile and compulsive deserter,
rescued again from its nothingness, from the depths of a misty
    landfill?

¿O será simplemente como escombro que se arroja y se olvida?
No, este cuerpo no puede ser tan sólo para entrar y salir.
Yo reclamo los ojos que guardaron el Etna bajo las ascuas de otros ojos;
pido por esta piel con la que caigo al fondo de cada precipicio;
abogo por las manos que buscaron, por los pies que perdieron;
apelo hasta por el luto de mi sangre y el hielo de mis huesos.
Aunque no haya descanso, ni permanencia, ni sabiduría.
defiendo mi lugar:
esta humilde morada donde el alma insondable se repliega.
donde inmola sus sombras
y se va.

Or will it be simply like rubbish thrown away and forgotten?
No, this body can't be only for entrances and exits.
I reclaim those eyes that watched Etna beneath the embers of other eyes;
I beg for this skin with which I fall to the bottom of each precipice;
I plead for the hands that searched, for the feet that got lost;
I appeal by my blood's mourning and my bones' ice.
Though there's no rest, no permanence, no wisdom,
I defend my place:
this humble home where my fathomless soul is folded,
where it sacrifices its shadows
and leaves.

LA ABUELA

Ella mira pasar desde su lejanía las vanas estaciones,
el ademán ligero con que idénticos días se despiden
dejando solo el eco, el rumor de otros días apagados
bajo la gran marea de su corazón.

De todos los que amaron ciertas edades suyas,
    ciertos gestos,
las mismas poblaciones con olor a leyenda,
no quedan más que nombres a los que a veces vuelven como a un sueño
cuando ella interroga con sus manos el apacible polvo de las cosas
que antaño recobrara de un larguísimo olvido.
Sí. Ese siempre tan lejos como nunca,
esa memoria apenas alcanzada, en un último esfuerzo,
por la costumbre de la piel o por la enorme sabiduría de la sangre.

Ella recorre aún la sombra de su vida,
el afán de otro tiempo, la imposible desdicha soportada;
y regresa otra vez,
otra vez todavía, desde el fondo de las profundas ruinas,
a su tierna paciencia, al cuerpo insostenible, a su vejez,
igual que a un aposento donde solo resuenan las pisadas
    de los antiguos huéspedes
que aguardan, en la noche, el último llamado de la tierra entreabierta.

Ella nos mira ya desde la verdadera realidad de su rostro.

THE GRANDMOTHER

From her distance she watches the vain seasons pass,
slight gesture with which identical days say goodbye over and over
leaving only the echo, rumor of other days
extinguished beneath her heart's great tide.

Nothing remains of all those who loved certain of her ages,
    certain gestures,
the very towns carrying the perfume of legends,
nothing but the names for those who sometimes return as if to a dream
when she questions with her hands the meek dust of things
she recovered yesterday from a long oblivion.
Yes. Always as far away as ever,
memory barely reached in a final effort,
through her skin's habit or her blood's enormous wisdom.

She still surveys the shadow of her life,
desire from an earlier time, impossible misfortune endured;
and again she returns,
and yet again, from the depth of deep ruins,
to her tender patience, to her untenable body, to her old age—
as if to a room where only the footsteps of former guests
    echo—
waiting, in the night, for the last call of the half-open earth.

She looks at us already from the true reality of her face.

IV

LLEGA EN CADA TORMENTA

¿Y no sientes acaso tú también un dolor tormentoso sobre la piel
    del tiempo,
como de cicatriz que vuelve a abrirse allí
donde fue descuajado de raíz el cielo?
¿Y no sientes a veces que aquella noche junta sus jirones
    en un ave agorera,
que hay un batir de alas contra el techo,
como un entrechocar de inmensas hojas de primavera en duelo
o de palmas que llaman a morir?
¿Y no sientes después que el expulsado llora,
que es un rescoldo de ángel caído en el umbral,
aventado de pronto igual que la mendiga por una ráfaga extranjera?
¿Y no sientes conmigo que pasa sobre ti
una casa que rueda hacia el abismo con un chocar de loza trizada
    por el rayo,
con dos trajes vacíos que se abrazan para un viaje sin fin,
con un chirriar de ejes que se quiebran de pronto como las rotas frases
    del amor?
¿Y no sientes entonces que tu lecho se hunde como la nave
    de una catedral arrastrada por la caída de los cielos,
y que un agua viscosa corre sobre tu cara hasta el juicio final?

Es otra vez el légamo.
De nuevo el corazón arrojado en el fondo del estanque,
prisionero de nuevo entre las ondas con que se cierra un sueño.

Tiéndete como yo en esta miserable eternidad de un día.
Es inútil aullar.
De estas aguas no beben las bestias del olvido.

IT COMES IN EVERY STORM

And don't you feel also, perhaps, a stormy sorrow on the skin
    of time,
like a scar that opens again
there where the sky was uprooted?
And don't you feel sometimes how that night gathers its tatters
    into an ominous bird,
that there's a beating of wings against the roof
like a clash among immense spring leaves struggling
or of hands clapping to summon you to death?
And don't you feel afterwards someone exiled is crying,
that there's an ember of a fallen angel on the threshold,
brought suddenly like a beggar by an alien gust of wind?
And don't you feel, like me, that a house rolling toward the abyss
runs over you with a crash of crockery shattered
    by lightning,
with two empty shells embracing each other for an endless journey,
with a screech of axles suddenly fractured like love's broken
    promises?
And don't you feel then your bed sinking like the nave of a cathedral
    crushed by the fall of heaven,
and that a thick, heavy water runs over your face till the final judgment?

Again it's the slime.
Again your heart thrown into the depth of the pool,
prisoner once more among the waves closing a dream.

Lie down as I do in this miserable eternity of one day.
It's useless to howl.
From these waters the beasts of oblivion don't drink.

EL OTRO LADO

No logras acertar con el lugar,
aunque te asista el sol y desciendan los cielos.
En seguida que llegas, como si se trocaran en vampiros las aves,
los mármoles en yeso y en polvorientas telas pintadas las praderas,
es una equivocación fatal la que te enfrenta con mirada de lobo
y te obliga a salir en cuatro pies, esquivando el castigo.
No es aquí ni es ahora,
grazna con las cornejas el viento que te aspira,
que te arrastra y revuelca como a un fardo de remolino en remolino
y te arroja por fin hacia un rincón en el que se adultera de nuevo
        el porvenir
entre los vidrios de la lejanía.
No es ese tu lugar, allí,
donde nadie te aguarda para nacer desde hace dos mil años
(ah, ese abrazo primero, semejante al abrazo de la resurrección),
donde no hay ni medida ni tiempo que se ajusten al hueco
        de tu mano
lo mismo que dos partes acuñadas para la alianza o la separación,
sencillamente igual a mitad y mitad,
como los dos costados de una misma medalla o las dos contrapartes
        para un crimen.
Nada. Palabras sin pronunciar, maniobras suspendidas,
ojos que aunque te sigan no te ven desde sus apariencias de ojos
        de retrato,
escenas atestadas de recuerdos ajenos para instalar otro destino,
y contra ti la piedra y la expulsión.
Fuera, fuera otra vez, con el miedo a la espalda,
frente al resto del mundo embellecido, otra vez centelleando,
otra vez aspirándote,
para la nueva prueba y el error.
¿Dónde será el lugar? ¿Dónde será otro lado?
O tú no eres de aquí o ese sitio no está en ninguna parte, todavía.
Aunque tal vez haya en alguna parte cerrada, inexpugnable, mentirosa,
una sombra ladrona probándose tu vida,
el otro lado.

THE OTHER SIDE

You can't find the place,
even though the sun helps you and the sky lowers.
As soon as you arrive, a fatal mistake confronts you with a wolf look
as if birds had turned into vampires,
marble into plaster and meadows into dusty wallpaper,
forcing you to crawl out on all fours to avoid punishment.
It's not here or now,
the wind that inhales you croaks with crows,
drags you and tumbles you around like a bundle from whirlwind
    to whirlwind,
and tosses you, at last, toward a corner where the future is diluted again
among the glass panes of the distance.
That isn't your place, there,
where no one has waited to be born for two thousand years
(ah, that first embrace, like the embrace of resurrection),
where there's neither measure nor time to fit into the hollow
    of your hand,
like two parts coined for union or separation,
simply equal to half and half,
like two sides of the same medal or two versions of one crime.
Nothing. Words not spoken, operations suspended,
eyes like the eyes in portraits that follow you though they don't
    see you,
scenes packed with alien memories installing another destiny,
and, against you, stone and expulsion.
Out, get out again, with fear at your back,
before the rest of the world, embellished,
shimmering once more,
once more breathing you in,
new trial and error.
Where can that place be? Where's the other side?
Either you aren't from here or that place isn't anywhere yet.
Even though perhaps there may be in some closed spot a thieving shadow,
unyielding, lying, trying on your life,
the other side.

VARIACIONES SOBRE EL TIEMPO

Tiempo:
te has vestido con la piel carcomida del último profeta;
te has gastado la cara hasta la extrema palidez;
te has puesto una corona hecha de espejos rotos y lluviosos jirones,
y salmodias ahora el balbuceo del porvenir con las desenterradas
    melodías de antaño,
mientras vagas en sombras por tu hambriento escorial,
    como los reyes locos.

No me importan ya nada todos tus desvaríos de fantasma inconcluso,
miserable anfitrión.
Puedes roer los huesos de las grandes promesas en sus desvencijados
    catafalcos
o paladear el áspero brebaje que rezuman las decapitaciones.
Y aún no habrá bastante,
hasta que no devores con tu corte goyesca la molienda final.

Nunca se acompasaron nuestros pasos en estos entrecruzados laberintos.
Ni siquiera al comienzo,
cuando me conducías de la mano por el bosque embrujado
y me obligabas a correr sin aliento detrás de aquella torre inalcanzable
o a descubrir siempre la misma almendra con su oscuro sabor
    de miedo y de inocencia.
¡Ah, tu plumaje azul brillando entre las ramas!
No pude embalsamarte ni conseguí extraer tu corazón
    como una manzana de oro.

Demasiado apremiante,
fuiste después el látigo que azuza,
el cochero imperial arrollándome entre las patas de sus bestias.
Demasiado moroso,
me condenaste a ser el rehén ignorado,
la víctima sepultada hasta los hombros entre siglos de arena.

VARIATIONS ON TIME

Time:
you've dressed in the moth-eaten skin of the last prophet;
you've worn down your face to its last pallor;
you've put on a crown of shattered mirrors and tatters of rain;
and now you chant babble about the future with melodies dug up
    from the past,
while you wander in the shadows through your starving rubbish,
    like a mad king.

All your ravings of a fragmented ghost no longer matter to me,
you wretched host.
You can gnaw the bones of great promises on their rickety
    biers,
or relish the bitter brew that oozes from the beheaded.
And even then there won't be enough
until you swallow the last grinding in your Goyaesque elegance.

Our steps through those tangled labyrinths never kept pace together.
Not even in the beginning,
when you led me by the hand through the bewitched forest,
and made me run breathless after that unattainable tower,
or made me discover always the same almond with its dark taste
    of fear and innocence.
Ah, your blue plumage shining among the branches!
I could not embalm you or extract your heart
    like a golden apple.

Later you were the whip that goads,
too cruel,
the imperial coachman rolling me up between the feet of his horses.
Too slow,
you condemned me to be the unknown hostage,
victim buried up to my neck in centuries of sand.

Hemos luchado a veces cuerpo a cuerpo.
Nos hemos disputado como fieras cada porción de amor,
cada pacto firmado con la tinta que fraguas
     en alguna instantánea eternidad,
cada rostro esculpido en la inconstancia de las nubes viajeras,
cada casa erigida en la corriente que no vuelve.
Lograste arrebatarme uno por uno esos desmenuzados fragmentos
     de mis templos.
No vacíes la bolsa.
No exhibas tus trofeos.
No relates de nuevo tus hazañas de vergonzoso gladiador
     en las desmesuradas galerías del eco.

Tampoco yo te concedí una tregua.
Violé tus estatutos.
Forcé tus cerraduras y subí a los graneros que denominan porvenir.
Hice una sola hoguera con todas tus edades.
Te volví del revés igual que a un maleficio que se quiebra,
o mezclé tus recintos como en un anagrama cuyas letras truecan
     el orden y cambian el sentido.
Te condensé hasta el punto de una burbuja inmóvil,
opaca, prisionera en mis vidriosos cielos.
Estiré tu piel seca en leguas de memoria,
hasta que la horadaron poco a poco los pálidos agujeros del olvido.
Algún golpe de dados te hizo vacilar sobre el vacío inmenso
     entre dos horas.

Hemos llegado lejos en este juego atroz, acorralándonos el alma.
Sé que no habrá descanso,
y no me tientas, no, con dejarme invadir por la plácida sombra
     de los vegetales centenarios,
aunque de nada me valga estar en guardia,
aunque al final de todo estés de pie, recibiendo tu paga,
el mezquino soborno que acuñan en tu honor las roncas maquinarias
     de la muerte,
mercenario.

Y no escribas entonces en las fronteras blancas "nunca más"
con tu mano ignorante,

Sometimes we've fought hand to hand.
We've struggled like wild beasts over each share of love,
over each pact signed with the ink you brew
        in some instantaneous eternity,
each face sculpted in the changing of fleeting clouds,
each house erected in the tide that never turns.
One by one you snatched from me the crumbled fragments
        of my temples.
Don't empty the purse.
Don't show off your trophies.
Don't tell me your deeds again like a shameful gladiator
        in the vast galleries of echo.

I never granted you a truce.
I broke your laws.
I forced your locks and climbed up to the storehouses called the future.
I made a single bonfire out of all your ages.
I turned you inside out like a broken spell
or mixed up your secret places as in an anagram whose letters
        change places and shift meaning.
I condensed you till you became a still bubble,
opaque, prisoner in my glass skies.
I stretched your dried skin over leagues of memory,
until, little by little, the pale holes of oblivion pierced it.
A toss of the dice made you pause above the immense void
        between two hours.

We've come a long way, rounding up our souls, in this atrocious game.
I know there'll be no rest,
and you can't tempt me, no, not with being invaded by the placid shade
        of age-old plants,
even though it does me no good to be on guard,
even though you stand there,
mercenary,
till the end of everything, receiving your wages,
mean bribe coined in your honor by the hoarse machinery of death.

And don't write "nevermore," then, on the white borders
with your ignorant hand,

como si fueras algún dios de Dios,
un guardián anterior, el amo de ti mismo en otro tú
      que colma las tinieblas.
Tal vez seas apenas la sombra más infiel de alguno de sus perros.

as if you were some god of God's,
a guardian from the past, master of yourself in another you that fills up
the darkness.
Perhaps you are only the most faithless shadow of one of his dogs.

OLGA OROZCO

Yo, Olga Orozco, desde tu corazón digo a todos que muero.
Amé la soledad, la heroica perduración de toda fe,
el ocio donde crecen animales extraños y plantas fabulosas,
la sombra de un gran tiempo que pasó entre misterios
     y entre alucinaciones,
y también el pequeño temblor de las bujías en el anochecer.
Mi historia está en mis manos y en las manos con que otros
     las tatuaron.
De mi estadía quedan las magias y los ritos,
unas fechas gastadas por el soplo de un despiadado amor,
la humareda distante de la casa donde nunca estuvimos,
y unos gestos dispersos entre los gestos de otros que no me conocieron.
Lo demás aún se cumple en el olvido,
aún labra la desdicha en el rostro de aquella que se buscaba en mí igual
     que en un espejo de sonrientes praderas,
y a la que tú verás extrañamente ajena:
mi propia aparecida condenada a mi forma de este mundo.
Ella hubiera querido guardarme en el desdén o en el orgullo,
en un último instante fulmíneo como el rayo,
no en el túmulo incierto donde alzo todavía la voz ronca y llorada
entre los remolinos de tu corazón.
No. Esta muerte no tiene descanso ni grandeza.
No puedo estar mirándola por primera vez durante tanto tiempo.
Pero debo seguir muriendo hasta tu muerte
porque soy tu testigo ante una ley más honda y más oscura
     que los cambiantes sueños,
allá, donde escribimos la sentencia:
"Ellos han muerto ya.
Se habían elegido por castigo y perdón, por cielo y por infierno.
Son ahora una mancha de humedad en las paredes del primer aposento".

OLGA OROZCO

I, Olga Orozco, tell everyone, from your heart, I'm dying.
I loved solitude, the heroic endurance of all faith,
leisure where strange animals and fabulous plants grow,
the shadow of a great age that moved between mysteries
        and hallucinations,
and also the slight trembling of lamps in the dusk.
My story rests in my hands and in the hands of those who tattooed
        them.
From my sojourn, magic and rites remain,
and a few anniversaries worn by the gust from a cruel love,
distant smoke from the house where we never lived,
and gestures scattered among the gestures of people who never knew me.
All the rest is still unfolding in oblivion,
still carving grief on the face of the woman who sought herself in me, as
        in a mirror of smiling meadows,
the one you'll consider strangely alien:
my ghost, condemned to my form in this world.
She would have liked to regard me with scorn or pride,
at the last instant, like a flash of lightning,
not in the confused tomb where I still raise my hoarse voice, tearful
among the whirlwinds of your heart.
No. This death admits no rest, no grandeur.
I cannot keep looking at it as I have for so long, as if for the first time.
But I must go on dying until your death
because I am your witness before a law deeper and darker
        than shifting dreams,
there, where we write the sentence:
"They are already dead.
They were chosen for punishment and pardon, for heaven and hell.
Now they are a damp spot on the walls of their first home."

V

LAS MUERTES

He aquí unos muertos cuyos huesos no blanqueará la lluvia,
lápidas donde nunca ha resonado el golpe tormentoso de la piel
    del lagarto,
inscripciones que nadie recorrerá encendiendo la luz de alguna lágrima;
arena sin pisadas en todas las memorias.
Son los muertos sin flores.
No nos legaron cartas, ni alianzas, ni retratos.
Ningún trofeo heroico atestigua la gloria o el oprobio.
Sus vidas se cumplieron sin honor en la tierra,
mas su destino fue fulmíneo como un tajo;
porque no conocieron ni el sueño ni la paz en los infames lechos
    vendidos por la dicha,
porque sólo acataron una ley más ardiente que la ávida gota
    de salmuera.
Ésa y no cualquier otra.
Ésa y ninguna otra.
Por eso es que sus muertes son los exasperados rostros de nuestra vida.

THE DEATHS

Look at some dead whose bones the rain will not whiten,
tombstones where the stormy blow of lizard skin has never
    resounded,
inscriptions nobody will scan lighting the light of some tear;
sand without footprints in every memory.
They are the dead with no flowers.
They did not bequeath us letters, or wedding rings, or portraits.
No heroic trophy testifies to their glory or ignominy.
Their lives were completed without honor on earth,
but their destiny was as explosive as a knife flash;
because they knew neither dreams nor peace in the infamous beds
    betrayed by happiness,
because they only obeyed a law more ardent than the avid drop
    of brine.
That law and no other.
That and that alone.
That is why their deaths are the exasperated faces of our life.

BALADA DE LOS LUGARES OLVIDADOS

Mis refugios más bellos,
los lugares que se adaptan mejor a los colores últimos de mi alma,
están hechos de todo lo que los otros olvidaron.

Son sitios solitarios excavados en la caricia de la hierba,
en una sombra de alas; en una canción que pasa;
regiones cuyos límites giran con los carruajes fantasmales
que transportan la niebla en el amanecer
y en cuyos cielos se dibujan nombres, viejas frases de amor,
juramentos ardientes como constelaciones de luciérnagas ebrias.

Algunas veces pasan poblaciones terrosas, acampan roncos trenes,
una pareja junta naranjas prodigiosas en el borde del mar,
una sola reliquia se propaga por toda la extensión.
Parecerían espejismos rotos,
recortes de fotografías arrancados de un álbum para orientar
     a la nostalgia,
pero tienen raíces más profundas que este suelo que se hunde,
estas puertas que huyen, estas paredes que se borran.

Son islas encantadas en las que sólo yo puedo ser la hechicera.

¿Y quién si no, sube las escaleras hacia aquellos desvanes
     entre nubes
donde la luz zumbaba enardecida en la miel de la siesta,
vuelve a abrir el arcón donde yacen los restos de una historia
     inclemente,
mil veces inmolada nada más que a delirios, nada más que a espumas,
y se prueba de nuevo los pedazos
como aquellos disfraces de las protagonistas invencibles,
el círculo de fuego con el que encandilaba al escorpión del tiempo?

¿Quién limpia con su aliento los cristales y remueve la lumbre
     del atardecer
en aquellas habitaciones donde la mesa era un altar de idolatría,

BALLAD OF FORGOTTEN PLACES

My most beautiful hiding places,
places that best fit my soul's deepest colors,
are made of all that others forgot.

They are solitary sites hollowed out in the grass's caress,
in a shadow of wings, in a passing song;
regions whose limits swirl with the ghostly carriages
that transport the mist in the dawn,
and in whose skies names are sketched, ancient words of love,
vows burning like constellations of drunken fireflies.

Sometimes earthy villages pass, hoarse trains make camp,
a couple piles marvelous oranges at the edge of the sea,
a single relic is spread through all space.
My places would look like broken mirages,
clippings of photographs torn from an album to orient
        nostalgia,
but they have roots deeper than this sinking ground,
these fleeing doors, these vanishing walls.

They are enchanted islands where only I can be the magician.

And who else, if not I, is climbing the stairs toward those attics
        in the clouds
where the light, aflame, used to hum in the siesta's honey,
who else will open again the big chest where the remains
        of an unhappy story lie,
sacrificed a thousand times only to fantasy, only to foam,
and try on the rags again
like those costumes of invincible heroes,
circle of fire that inflamed time's scorpion?

Who cleans the windowpane with her breath and stirs the fire
        of the afternoon
in those rooms where the table was an altar of idolatry,

cada silla, un paisaje replegado después de cada viaje,
y el lecho, un tormentoso atajo hacia la otra orilla de los sueños;
aposentos profundos como redes suspendidas del cielo,
como los abrazos sin fin donde me deslizaba hasta rozar las plumas
     de la muerte,
hasta invertir las leyes del conocimiento y la caída?

¿Quién se interna en los parques con el soplo dorado de cada Navidad
y lava los follajes con un trapito gris que fue el pañuelo
     de las despedidas,
y entrelaza de nuevo las guirnaldas con un hilo de lágrimas,
repitiendo un fantástico ritual entre copas trizadas y absortos
     comensales,
mientras paladea en las doce uvas verdes de la redención
—una por cada mes, una por cada año, una por cada siglo
     de vacía indulgencia—
un ácido sabor menos mordiente que el del pan del olvido?

¿Porque quién sino yo les cambia el agua a todos los recuerdos?
¿Quién incrusta el presente como un tajo entre las proyecciones
     del pasado?
¿Alguien trueca mis lámparas antiguas por sus lámparas nuevas?

Mis refugios más bellos son sitios solitarios a los que nadie va
y en los que sólo hay sombras que se animan cuando soy la hechicera.

each chair, a landscape folded up after every trip,
and the bed, a stormy short cut to the other shore of dreams,
rooms deep as nets hung from the sky,
like endless embraces I slid down till I brushed the feathers
    of death,
until I overturned the laws of knowledge and the fall of man?

Who goes into the parks with the golden breath of each Christmas
and washes the foliage with a little gray rag that was the handkerchief
    for waving goodbye,
and reweaves the garlands with a thread of tears,
repeating a fantastic ritual among smashed wine glasses and guests lost
    in thought,
while she savors the twelve green grapes of redemption—
one for each month, one for each year, one for each century
    of empty indulgence—
a taste acid but not as sharp as the bread of forgetfulness?

Because who but I changes the water for all the memories?
Who inserts the present like a slash into the dreams
    of the past?
Who switches my ancient lamps for new ones?

My most beautiful hiding places are solitary sites where no one goes,
and where there are shadows that only come to life when I am
    the magician.

MURO DE LOS LAMENTOS

Paso a paso a lo largo de la pared que fue visión tramposa,
transparencia entreabierta,
y ahora está cerrada como boca cerrada
—como estarán cerrados los oídos de mis sobrevivientes al reclamo
     obstinado—,
por más que me deslice con persuasión de aroma a sigilo de lluvia
contra la torva piedra,
que tal vez sólo tenga nostalgia de mi frente reclinada en su noche,
en la blancura inmensa.
¡Ah desierto insoluble con su enigma de pie como la esfinge
     que me acosa!
Siempre hay una pared fatal que se adelanta cuando yo me asomo,
un escollo insalvable fabricado con saña en todos los talleres
     del destino
para que no me jacte de ninguna victoria sobre el polvo,
para que nunca olvide la distancia que media entre la sed y el vaso,
entre el relámpago y el trueno.
Siempre hay una pared que me rechaza, que me arroja a las fieras
o desvía mis pies hacia lugares donde no puedo entrar
     o adonde nunca llego
y en los que sin embargo estará envejeciendo la primavera que me sueña
"Apágate, confuso resplandor, polilla encandilada;
no hay sitio para guardar tanta intemperie detrás de un solo muro",
alguien dice, alguien grazna como la bruja de medianoche en el tejado.
Y la estatura de la prohibición asciende, se agiganta y rebasa,
cubre hasta el cielo en nombre de un demonio.
Feroz, insobornable, la guardiana.
A veces me persigue hasta en los sueños esta infernal mampostería.
¿No será que yo llevo esta pared conmigo?

WAILING WALL

Step by step I slide along the wall that was a deceptive sight,
transparency ajar,
but now is sealed tight as a shut mouth.
So the ears of my survivors will be closed to my obstinate
        call—
whether I slide with the subtlety of an aroma or the stealth of rain
on harsh stone
that barely misses, perhaps, my forehead leaning against its night,
in the immense whiteness.
What an unknowable desert with its enigma crouching like the sphinx
        who haunts me!
There's always a fatal wall that advances when I appear,
an insurmountable obstacle made with fury in all of destiny's
        workshops
so I won't brag of victory over dust,
so I'll never forget the distance that stretches between thirst and glass,
lightning and thunder.
There's always a wall that repels me, throws me to the beasts,
or turns my feet aside toward places I can't enter or never
        get to
and where even so the springtime that dreams me is growing old.
"Turn yourself off, blurred glitter, dazzled moth,
there's no room to keep so much homelessness behind a single wall,"
someone says, someone croaks like the midnight witch on the roof.
And the form of the prohibition swells, rises, and sails past,
covers up even the sky in the name of a demon.
Ferocious, incorruptible, my guardian.
Sometimes this infernal stonework pursues me even in my dreams.
Is that because I carry this wall within me?

EN EL FINAL ERA EL VERBO

Como si fueran sombras de sombras que se alejan las palabras,
humaredas errantes exhaladas por la boca del viento,
así se me dispersan, se me pierdan de vista contra las puertas del silencio.
Son menos que las últimas borras de un color, que un suspiro en la hierba;
fantasmas que ni siquiera se asemejan al reflejo que fueron.
Entonces ¿no habrá nada que se mantenga en su lugar,
nada que se confunda con su nombre desde la piel hasta los huesos?
Y yo que me cobijaba en las palabras como en los pliegues
        de la revelación
o que fundaba mundos de visiones sin fondo para sustituir los jardines
        del edén
sobre las piedras del vocablo.
¿Y no he intentado acaso pronunciar hacia atrás todos los alfabetos
        de la muerte?
¿No era ese tu triunfo en las tinieblas, poesía?
Cada palabra a imagen de otra luz, a semejanza de otro abismo,
cada una con su cortejo de constelaciones, con su nido de víboras,
pero dispuesta a tejer y a destejer desde su propio costado el universo
y a prescindir de mí hasta el última nudo.
Extensiones sin límites plegadas bajo el signo de un ala,
urdimbres como andrajos para dejar pasar el soplo alucinante
        de los dioses,
reversos donde el misterio se desnuda,
donde arroja uno a uno los sucesivos velos, los sucesivos nombres,
sin alcanzar jamás el corazón cerrado de la rosa.
Yo velaba incrustada en el ardiente hielo, en la hoguera escarchada,
traduciendo relámpagos, desenhebrando dinastías de voces,
bajo un código tan indescifrable como el de las estrellas
        o el de las hormigas.
Miraba las palabras al trasluz.
Veía desfilar sus oscuras progenies hasta el final del verbo.
Quería descubrir a Dios por transparencia.

IN THE END WAS THE WORD

So my words scatter—
as if they were shadows of shadows that withdraw,
billows of wandering smoke exhaled by the wind's mouth—
vanishing from my sight behind the doors of silence.
They are less than the last lees of a color, than a sigh in the grass;
ghosts that don't even resemble the reflection they once were.
Won't anything, then, stay in its place, won't anything
merge with its name from skin to bone?
And I who took cover in words as if in the folds of revelation,
who built worlds of endless visions to put the garden
  of Eden
on the stones of the word!
Haven't I tried to say all of death's alphabets
  backwards?
Poetry, wasn't that your triumph over the darkness?
Each word in the image of another light, in the image of another abyss,
each word with its following of constellations, its vipers' nest,
yet seeking to weave and unweave the universe from its own rib
and to dispense with me even to the last knot.
Limitless spaces folded beneath the sign of a wing,
intrigues like tatters to let the hallucinatory sigh
  of the gods pass,
the other side where mystery is bared,
where, one by one, it casts off successive veils, successive names,
without ever reaching the closed heart of the rose.
I kept watch encrusted in burning ice, in frosted fire,
translating lightning, unthreading dynasties of words,
in a code as indecipherable as that of stars
  or ants.
I looked at words against the light.
I saw their dark offspring parade by till the end of the word.
I wanted to discover God in transparency.

CHRONOLOGICAL PLACEMENT OF POEMS
IN OROZCO'S WORK

from *Desde lejos*, 1946:
Far Away, From My Hill, p. 19
A Face in Autumn, p. 51
After Days, p. 57
The Grandmother, p. 67

from *Las muertes*, 1952:
The Stranger, p. 61
Olga Orozco, p. 81
The Deaths, p. 85

from *Los juegos peligrosos*, 1962:
To Make a Talisman, p. 47
It Comes in Every Storm, p. 71
To Destroy the Enemy, p. 37

from *Museo salvaje*, 1974:
Personal Stamp, p. 15
Some Feathers for My Wings, p. 23

from *Cantos a Berenice*, 1977
Songs to Berenice, II, p. 27

from *Mutaciones de la realidad*, 1979:
Vampire Continent, p. 29
I Row Against the Night, p. 41
Variations on Time, p. 75

from *La noche a la deriva*, 1983:
Omen, p. 35
Ballad of Forgotten Places, p. 87

from *En el revés del cielo,* 1987:
    Animal Catechism, p. 63
    The Other Side, p. 73
    Wailing Wall, p. 91
    In the End Was the Word, p. 93

from *Con esta boca, en este mundo,* 1994:
    Les Jeux Sont Faits, p. 53

ACKNOWLEDGMENTS

The poems in this book have previously appeared in the following magazines:

American Poetry Review: "It Comes in Every Storm" and "Far Away, from My Hill";
The American Voice: "Animal Catechism";
Artful Dodge: "Omen";
Beacons: "The Grandmother";
The Black Warrior Review: "After Days";
Bomb: "Songs to Berenice, II";
Graham House Review: "Vampire Continent";
International Poetry Review: "The Stranger";
Many Mountains Moving: "A Face in Autumn";
Mid-American Review: "I Row Against the Night";
Mr. Knife, Miss Fork: "The Deaths" and "*Les Jeux Sont Faits*";
Quarry West: "Some Feathers for My Wings";
Review: Latin American Art and Literature: "To Destroy the Enemy" and "Ballad of Forgotten Places";
Seneca Review: "Personal Stamp" and "To Make a Talisman."

"Variations on Time" and "I Row Against the Night" first appeared in *Woman Who Has Sprouted Wings: Poems by Contemporary Latin American Women Poets*, ed. Mary Crow (Latin American Literary Review Press, 1987).

"Animal Catechism" was reprinted from *The American Voice* for *The American Voice Anthology of Poetry 1998*, American Voice Literary Magazine, 1998.

ABOUT THE AUTHOR

Olga Orozco (1920–1999) is one of the most important contemporary poets of Argentina and arguably the most important contemporary woman poet of Latin America. In more than a dozen books, starting with *Desde lejos* (*From Far Away*) in 1946, Olga Orozco created a coherent body of work with a clearly recognizable poetic voice and a Surrealist style that draws together imagery from the occult and daily life. Her principal collections of poems include *Las muertes* (*The Deaths*, 1951), *Los juegos peligrosos* (*Dangerous Games*, 1962), *Museo salvaje* (*Wild Museum*, 1974), *Cantos a Berenice* (*Songs to Berenice*, 1977), *Mutaciones de la realidad* (*Mutations of Reality*, 1979), *La noche a la deriva* (*Night Adrift*, 1984), *En el revés del cielo* (*On the Other Side of the Sky*, 1987), and *Con esta boca, en este mundo* (*With This Mouth, In This World*, 1992). In addition, a half dozen volumes of her selected poems have appeared and two collections of her short stories. International recognition of her work has led to its translation into French, English, Italian, German, Rumanian, Hindi, Portuguese, and Japanese.

ABOUT THE TRANSLATOR

Mary Crow is the author of three previous works of translation as well as five collections of her own poems. In 1992 she published *Vertical Poetry: Recent·Poems of Roberto Juarroz* (White Pine Press), which won a Colorado Book Award; in 1990, *From the Country of Nevermore: Poems by Jorge Teillier* (Wesleyan University Press); and in 1987, *Woman Who Has Sprouted Wings: Poems by Contemporary Latin American Women Poets* (Latin American Literary Review Press), which won a Translation Award from Columbia University's Translation Center. Recently, her translations of poems by Roberto Juarroz and Enrique Lihn appeared in the anthologies *The Vintage Book of Contemporary World Poetry* (Vintage, 1996), edited by J.D. McClatchy, and *The Poetry of Our World*, edited by Jeffrey Paine (HarperCollins, 2002). She serves as Poet Laureate of Colorado and teaches in the Creative Writing Program at Colorado State University.

Lannan Translation Selections 2002

Ljuba Merlina Bortolani, *The Siege* (*L'Assedio*)

Olga Orozco, *Engravings Torn From Insomnia*

For more on the Lannan Translations Selection Series
visit our Web site:
www.boaeditions.org

Colophon

The publication of this book was made possible by the special
support of the following individuals:

Debra Audet
Laure-Anne Bosselaar & Kurt Brown
Nancy & Alan Cameros
Dr. Henry & Beverly French
Suzanne & Gerard Gouvernet
Kip & Deb Hale
Peter & Robin Hursh
Robert & Willy Hursh
Dorothy & Henry Hwang
Paul & Serena Kusserow
Archie & Pat Kutz
Mark Irwin
Boo Poulin
Deborah Ronnen
Jane Schuster
Pat & Michael Wilder
Sabra & Clifton Wood

* * *

Engravings Torn from Insomnia by Olga Orozco
was set in Goudy fonts
with Monotype Arabesque Ornaments
by Richard Foerster of York Beach, Maine.
The cover design is by Jean Brunel, New York, New York.
The cover art, "M. in the Water" is by Roberto Lebron.
Manufacturing was by McNaughton & Gunn, Saline, Michigan.

www.ingramcontent.com/pod-product-compliance
Lightning Source LLC
Jackson TN
JSHW080853211224
75817JS00002B/27